Sloths

FIRST EDITION

Editors Sally Beets, Kritika Gupta; **US Senior Editor** Shannon Beatty; **Designer** Bettina Myklebust Stovne;
Project Art Editor Rashika Kachroo; **Assistant Art Editor** Shubhi Srivastava; **Jacket Coordinator** Issy Walsh;
Jacket Designer Dheeraj Arora; **DTP Designers** Dheeraj Singh, Vikram Singh;
Picture Researcher Aditya Katyal; **Producer, Pre-Production** Dragana Puvacic; **Producer** Basia Ossowska;
Managing Editors Laura Gilbert, Monica Saigal; **Deputy Managing Art Editor** Ivy Sengupta;
Managing Art Editor Diane Peyton Jones; **Delhi Team Head** Malavika Talukder;
Creative Director Helen Senior; **Publishing Director** Sarah Larter;
Reading Consultant Linda Gambrell, PhD; **Subject Consultant** David Curnick

THIS EDITION

Editorial Management by Oriel Square
Produced for DK by WonderLab Group LLC
Jennifer Emmett, Erica Green, Kate Hale, *Founders*

Editors Grace Hill Smith, Libby Romero, Michaela Weglinski;
Photography Editors Kelley Miller, Annette Kiesow, Nicole DiMella; **Managing Editor** Rachel Houghton;
Designers Project Design Company; **Researcher** Michelle Harris; **Copy Editor** Lori Merritt;
Indexer Connie Binder; **Proofreader** Larry Shea; **Reading Specialist** Dr. Jennifer Albro;
Curriculum Specialist Elaine Larson

Published in the United States by DK Publishing
1745 Broadway, 20th Floor, New York, NY 10019

Copyright © 2023 Dorling Kindersley Limited
DK, a Division of Penguin Random House LLC
23 24 25 26 10 9 8 7 6 5 4 3 2 1
001–333985–June/2023

A catalog record for this book
is available from the Library of Congress.
HC ISBN: 978-0-7440-7318-8
PB ISBN: 978-0-7440-7319-5

DK books are available at special discounts when purchased in bulk for sales promotions, premiums, fundraising, or educational use. For details, contact: DK Publishing Special Markets,
1745 Broadway, 20th Floor, New York, NY 10019
SpecialSales@dk.com

Printed and bound in China

The publisher would like to thank the following for their kind permission to reproduce their images:
a=above; c=center; b=below; l=left; r=right; t=top; b/g=background

naturepl.com: Daniel Heuclin 20-21br

Cover images: *Front:* **Dreamstime.com:** Amplion b/g; **Shutterstock.com:** Lukas Kovarik cb;
Back: **Shutterstock.com:** Dasha D cra; *Spine:* **Dreamstime.com:** Amplion; **Shutterstock.com:** Lukas Kovarik b

All other images © Dorling Kindersley
For more information see: www.dkimages.com

For the curious
www.dk.com

Sloths

Laura Buller

DK

Contents

6   Let's Meet the Sloths

12   Growing Up

20   Slow and Sleepy

26   Sloth Survival

30   Glossary

31   Index

32   Quiz

Let's Meet the Sloths

Shhhhh! This little baby is asleep. It hangs on to its mother's fur as it snoozes. Mom is sound asleep, too. These sleepy mammals are sloths.

Zzzzz...

Zzzzz...

Sloths live high up in the trees in Central and South America. They hardly ever come down! There are plenty of leaves, buds, and shoots for these vegetarians to eat.

Sloths move very slowly. This makes it hard for other animals to spot them in the trees.

Green Fur

Sometimes, small plants called algae grow on sloth fur. This can make their fur turn green! A sloth's green fur blends in with the leaves.

bud

arm

claws

Long, curved claws help sloths to hang from trees.

Sloths hide by living high in the trees. They hang for hours using their long arms. Sloths' organs are attached to their bones. This means the organs won't squash their lungs when sloths dangle upside down from trees.

Growing Up

Squeak! A baby sloth talks to its mom. It holds on to her front, not her back like other animals. Mom and baby stay together for a whole year or more. The little one licks some food scraps from around the mom's mouth. Soon, it will munch its own meals.

Moms and babies stay together, but most adult sloths live alone.

baby

The mother sloth shows her baby how to climb through the treetops. Claws and strong muscles give sloths a good grip.

good grip on the branch

Mostly, the baby gives its mom an all-day hug.
Oops! Sometimes the little sloth slips off. However, it climbs back up again.

Once a week, sloths leave their treetop homes. They climb down to the forest floor to poop. The sloths crawl around. Their long claws make walking tricky. Their back legs are not very strong.

Splash! Sloths drop right into the water from the trees. Their long arms make them good swimmers.

They speed through the water more quickly than they move on land. After a swim, it's time for more sleeping.

The sloth swims using a stroke similar to the doggy paddle.

Slow and Sleepy

Don't ask a sloth to slow down. They are the slowest-moving mammals around! Up in the trees, they rarely move faster than seven feet (215 cm) per minute.

Sloths hardly ever come down to the ground.

On the ground, they are even slower. They crawl about one foot (30 cm) a minute. They move slowly to save energy.

Hanging Around

Sloths can sleep even while hanging upside down.

Sleeping so much helps sloths save energy, too. Sloths are among the biggest snoozers in the animal kingdom. Wild sloths nap for around 10 hours a day. In zoos, they sleep for as much as 15 hours.

Sloths are sleepy and slow because of what they eat. Leaves don't give them enough energy to zip around quickly. It takes sloths a month to digest one meal. You can do that in a day.

Leaves sit in a sloth's stomach for a very long time.

Sloth Survival

Sloths must be extra careful when they visit the forest floor. Jaguars and pumas are on the prowl. Sloths cannot run away from danger. They can only swipe their claws at predators to defend themselves. Then they can climb back up tree branches to escape.

puma

jaguar

Sloths are at risk in other ways, too. People are cutting down the trees where sloths live. Tourists can damage habitats. This had led to the pygmy sloth species nearly dying out.

Some sloth habitats have been destroyed.

Baby sloths at the Sloth Sanctuary in Costa Rica.

There are still people looking out for sloths. They want to protect them. Hopefully more sloths can sleep safely for many years to come.

Sweet dreams!

Algae
A simple, green plant that does not flower and grows on sloth fur

Claw
A curved nail on the toes of a bird, lizard, or mammal

Habitat
The home or environment where an animal lives

Mammal
A warm-blooded animal that has fur and makes milk to feed its young

Predator
An animal that hunts other animals for food

Rainforest
A lush, dense forest found in tropical areas that have heavy rainfall

Species
A type of animal or plant with shared features that can produce young together

Vegetarian
An animal that does not eat meat

Index

algae 8

arms 10, 11

baby sloth 6, 12–15, 29

buds 8, 9

Central America 8

claws 11, 14, 16

eating 8, 12, 25

forests 16, 26

fur 6, 8

green fur 8

habitats 28

jaguars 26, 27

leaves 8, 25

poop 16

predators 26

pumas 26, 27

pygmy sloth 28

sleep 6, 19, 22, 25

South America 8

speed 19, 20–21

survival 26–29

swimming 18–19

trees 8, 11, 18, 20, 26, 28

vegetarians 8

Quiz

Answer the questions to see what you have learned. Check your answers in the key below.

1.   How many hours a day can a sloth sleep?

2.   Why do sloths leave the treetops?

3.   What do sloths mainly eat?

4.   Why do sloths move slowly?

5.   Where do sloths move faster, on land or in water?

1. 10 to 15 hours a day 2. To poop 3. Leaves, buds, and shoots
4. Because of what they eat 5. In water